IMAGINE
Self-Love

A Journal

FROM BESTSELLING AUTHOR

Reba Linker

Get a Free Self-Love Discovery Session

Your relationship with yourself is, without a doubt, the most important relationship in your life. How you *treat yourself* 'sets the dial' for your relationships with everything else in your life:

- ❖ How much *wealth* do you allow into your life?
- ❖ How much *love* is right for you?
- ❖ How much *success* do you permit yourself to experience?
- ❖ What level of *vitality* is good enough for you?
- ❖ How much *happiness* can you imagine for yourself?

Get a free 30-minute Self-Love Discovery Session with transformational life coach and author Reba Linker, and see how boosting the dial on your 'self-love meter' can impact your life.

Get your free Self-Love Discovery Session here:
www.rebalinker.com/free-consultation/

This is a limited time offer.
Get the support you deserve.

.

Limits of Liability and Disclaimer of Warranty

The purpose of this book is to educate and entertain. The author and/or publisher do not guarantee that anyone following these techniques, suggestions, tips, ideas, or strategies will become successful. The author and/or publisher shall have neither liability nor responsibility to anyone with respect to any loss or damage caused, or alleged to be caused, directly or indirectly by the information contained in this book.

It is illegal to copy this book, post it to a website, or distribute it by any other means without permission from the publisher. No portion of this book may be reproduced mechanically, electronically, or by any other means, including photocopying, without written permission of the author, except in the case of brief quotations embodied in critical articles and reviews. Please do not participate or encourage piracy of copyrighted material in violation of the author's rights.

Imagine Self-Love
Reba Linker
An Earth & Sky Book

www.RebaLinker.com

Table of Contents

The contributions of my advance readers have been crucial to the development of this journal. A big thank you to Becky Lyter McCleery, Keyra Conlinn, Laurie Calkhoven, Dan Teck, Debbie Goldstein, and my darling husband, Franklin Linker.

I give thanks to a wonderful group of women who walked the path of the journal early in its development. It was beautiful to see the material come to life in their hands. Their enthusiasm and input contributed enormously to the product you see today.

I dedicate this journal to them, and to men and women everywhere reclaiming their self-love and happiness.

INTRODUCTION

Our most important relationship is the one we have with ourselves. How we relate to ourselves sets the bar for how we relate to everything and everyone in our lives, and how everything relates to us.

The journal is designed to strengthen the core concepts that enable our dreams to flourish: self-knowledge, self-acceptance, and self-love. Using inspirational quotes, journal prompts, and action exercises, the journal will help you establish self-love as the most important habit in your life.

This journal was inspired by the journey I traveled while writing my book, *Follow the Yarn*. As my life lessons grew to outpace the knitting tips, I underwent a parallel transition from dance studio owner, to life coach and author. Writing helped me discover my true purpose. At last I was able to stand and say: I accept myself, and I know my worth. This is a precious gift, for in knowing my worth, I am also able to tell whoever needs to hear: you are infinitely valuable and deserving, and you, by dint of being human, are invited to experience the greatest happiness.

In *Follow the Yarn* I shared my *story*; in these pages I share my *experience*. I offer you the same gifts that were given to me, to support you on your journey of discovery. This journal will strengthen your 'happiness reflex' by helping you remember how beautiful, powerful and unconditionally loved you are.

Live your best life NOW. Happiness is not 'over there,' at the completion of some goal, happiness is here, now. Connect with happiness on every page of this journal, in every moment of every day. Happiness is available to you all the time, no matter what is happening in your life, and no matter what happened in the past.

The Quotes

Quotes from *Follow the Yarn* are used as starting points for reflection in this journal. My knitting teacher, Ann Sokolowski, who was the catalyst for *Follow the Yarn*, was speaking of yarn when she declared: "Your work is worth quality ingredients," however, her message applies not just to knitting, but to all of life.

Ann's compassion for others and her confidence in herself informed everything she did, and I want to share that message of love and confidence with you. Truth is everywhere – in Ann's case, it just happened to come wrapped in yarn!

The Journal Prompts

Following each quote is a Journal Prompt. For example, the first quote, "Your work is worth quality ingredients," is followed by a prompt encouraging you to reflect upon how you can support your efforts: "I deserve…"

Complete the prompt with whatever pops into mind: "I deserve love," for example. Then simply repeat the process, writing whatever comes to mind, for example: "I deserve a new jacket." Use the suggested prompt over and over, adding extra pages as needed. (You might want to use a separate notebook for the exercises.)

There are no right or wrong answers. Insights run the gamut from "I need to get to bed earlier in order to be more alert the next day," to "If I dream of being an artist, then I deserve the time, space, and materials for my art."

Allow whatever wants to bubble up to come to the surface. Withhold value judgments about what you are expressing. It is, truly, all good. Listening to and expressing our thoughts, rather than what we may believe we *should* or *shouldn't* be feeling or thinking, is a huge part of practicing self-love.

Write! Scribble! Repeat yourself! Axe the censor and the editor! Let it flow! A thought on paper takes on a new life - so different from keeping it cooped up inside. Let it out!

It might help to set a timer for 10 or 20 minutes and challenge yourself to keep writing until it rings, or determine to fill a certain number of pages. Once you prime the pump, the waters will start to flow, and there is life-sustaining nourishment in the flow that comes from within you.

The Action Steps

As wonderful as reflection and journaling are, nothing is as powerful as putting insights into practice. An Action Step follows each Journal Prompt to integrate the concepts into your life in a hands-on, tangible way.

For example, following the "I deserve…" prompt, the Action Step asks you to add something to your life that supports your efforts. It can be as simple as drinking more water, or taking care of an unpaid bill. When we know what we deserve, it becomes easier to know what we need: we can clear the decks of any extraneous details that do not serve us, and incorporate practices that increase our energy, joy and satisfaction.

The relationship between the Journal Prompts and the Action Steps may be direct, or may be a looser, more 'poetic' connection. Trust the process. Discover your own connections. Through the quotes and exercises, we are 'circling' self-love, approaching it from different angles, each angle a different facet of the same precious gem.

Using the Journal

It is helpful to keep a notebook as you go through these pages. Use *Imagine Self-Love* as a guide, and use as many notebook pages as you need for each exercise.

Move at the speed that feels right for you. Respect the flow of your energy. Allow ideas to 'rest' and take root. Quicker is not better; it takes time and repetition to establish a new habit.

There is no such thing as 'on time' when it comes to this journal. The very first Journal Prompt – "I deserve…" – could be used for a year with powerful results; that one exercise, alone, could radically change your life.

It is perfectly natural to like some exercises more than others. Your responses are really all that matter; they reveal more about the true subject of this journal: YOU.

There is no right or wrong way to use the journal; the only 'wrong' way would be to make yourself 'wrong' through self-criticism or self-doubt. Allow yourself the freedom to walk the path of this journal in your own way: skip steps, or do each in order, race through to the end, or dwell on a particular stop along the way.

Listen to what your soul is calling you to do. The journal is here for you. It's yours. Use it in the way that feels right for you.

Keepin' It Real

No esoteric exercises here; no special talents or training required. The journal sparks simple awareness, using everyday language and common sense exercises.

There is no magic involved, yet simple efforts add up; with a shift in perspective here and a new habit there, the results can be quite magical. Even one new insight could influence the whole of your life.

My Effort is My Success

Self-love means learning to support ourselves, and we begin by calling our 'effort' our 'success.' Whether you complete a single exercise or repeat the entire journal over and over, your effort is a magnificent and worthy accomplishment.

The idea that your effort, not your result, is the measure of your success, is a major paradigm shift. I see again and again in my coaching practice the burst of energy, accomplishment and happiness that follows upon making that shift. Our culture steers us to focus on results, rather than process, yet, ironically, that focus on results does not always produce the best results. In fact, the stress of chasing external markers of success can be a deterrent to accomplishment and happiness.

Nice things are, well, nice, yet the truth is that happiness is within. The only reliable form of happiness is that which is always available, independent of the outer picture of your life. Have it all, and get it all, just know that what you seek is within YOU. This journal is here to help you uncover your magnificent nature, and to trust your essential joy. Your joy is always there, waiting for you.

What?! Me, Happy?!

The exercises may ring alarm bells for some who see the "I deserve..." type of journal prompt as 'selfish,' 'arrogant' or 'grabby.' This is totally understandable. Many of us feel uncomfortable with the idea of claiming what we desire. We are taught not to 'boast,' and to 'give, rather than receive.' It can be challenging to overcome those prohibitions.

It is vital that we get past our inner censor. I hold that it is natural for us to like (and even love) ourselves, to speak well of ourselves, and to treat ourselves with kindness, respect and compassion. It can take courage to claim our deservingness; declaring our own right to be happy may be the bravest thing we ever do.

That said, if claiming your entitlement still feels impossibly uncomfortable, then start by doing it for others. As the airline instruction says: "Parents of small children must put on their own oxygen masks, before helping children with their masks." When you take care of yourself you will be better able to nourish others in your life.

Imagine you being a top priority – and everyone around you loving it! Cool, huh?!

An Invitation

You already know, deep inside, what it means to be self-loving, to be gentle, patient, and forgiving of yourself. This journal is here to bring that practice of self-love to the forefront, and to lift it to the level of importance it deserves.

To the best of your ability, embody self-love as you walk the path of the journal. Hold on to self-love as you negotiate the inevitable bumps in the road that arise whenever we do any kind of work on ourselves.

Forgiveness, acceptance, tolerance, patience, kindness, and generosity *toward the self*: these are the hallmarks of self-love. Even more than any specific exercise, practice self-love in your approach to the journal, for when you practice self-love in one area, it becomes easier to apply the same principles in all other areas of your life.

What Do I Really Need to Be Happy?

Self-love teaches us what we *really* need to be happy. The airlines tell us that we need oxygen first in order to help our children; what do we need not just to survive, but to thrive? We can start by asking ourselves:

❖ What do I wish for, and how can I support that desire?

❖ How do I want to interact with the others in my life?

❖ What would bring me true and lasting happiness?

This journal will help you, like a loving friend, to see yourself with eyes of kindness, to fully see the good in yourself, and in others. You are so beautiful.

Writing *Follow the Yarn* led me to greater self-love. Now I am following the yarn further. It has led me here, to this journal, and to you. Where will *your* journey of self-love lead you?

❖ True happiness: knowing that you are perfect, just as you are.

❖ True joy: accepting and loving yourself, just as you are.

❖ True fulfillment: claiming happiness and joy as your birthright.

Blessings, *Reba*

"Your work is worth quality ingredients."

Journal Prompt: I deserve…

In the privacy of this journal let's allow ourselves to speak the truth of our souls. Many of us have been taught to be humble, to think of others first, to hold back from claiming what we desire.

In here, let's go for it! Let's invite the inner critic to wait outside – we have a job to do! And what a blissfully rewarding challenge it can be. Like watering a thirsty plant, see the leaves fill with vitality and color, see the stem lift and straighten!

Only a nourished plant yields bountiful fruit. A plant needs sunlight, water and air; what do YOU need in order to bring your dreams to fruition? Everyone's answers will be different – the common thread is our courage in allowing ourselves to speak our truth. Whatever you write - each and every answer is the correct answer.

I deserve _____

I deserve _____

I deserve _____

Use this space to keep writing (use additional pages as needed):

ACTION STEP:

CREATE A RITUAL

By the word 'ritual' I do not mean anything metaphysical, just simply an action that can become a new supportive habit in your daily life. Some ideas could be:

❖ Give yourself some quiet time. It could be a moment of reflection before you start your day, or a mid-day treat: choose a quiet spot, shut off your phones and other devices, and give yourself the gift of just *being*.

❖ Make a healthful salad or stir-fry; take the time and intention to nourish yourself.

❖ Make a habit of giving yourself gifts on a regular basis. The size of the gift is unimportant – it could be a cappuccino, or a hand-picked wildflower, or some pretty stationery – what matters is that it pleases you.

❖ Reach out to a friend who makes you feel good.

❖ Create a going-to-bed ritual: take the time and care to lay out a special outfit for the next day, do some gentle stretching, take a soothing bath, etc.

Give yourself something that you do not usually allow yourself. We get so busy taking care of others; taking a simple action for ourselves can feel totally awesome!

Use this space to journal about your experience with this Action Step:

"Know what is worth your time and craftsmanship — and what is not."

Journal Prompt: What I love about myself is…

Only when we *love* ourselves do we fully *value* ourselves.

Go for it. Set a timer and write, without censoring your words. What do YOU love about yourself? Is it the same as what other people love about you, or is it different? Write as much as possible, and about as many different aspects of yourself as you can.

In this, and in every exercise, feel free to modify the journal prompt for your comfort and ease in writing, as in the examples, below. Use slight variations in phrase to stimulate new responses.

What I love about myself is _____

What is so lovable about me is _____

I love my _____

Use this space to keep writing (use additional pages as needed):

ACTION STEP:

WHAT IS WORTHY OF YOU?

What activities are worthy of your time and energy?

Think about your day, and notice the things you love to do, and those that are more of a 'chore.' Just notice.

Once you have noticed, ask yourself:

How can I put more energy into the things I love?

And…

How can I eliminate, delegate, re-organize or re-energize the things I do not care to do?

Right now, choose one small change that shifts the balance of your day toward that which gives you joy. This is so individual. It may mean creating time for your art or hobby, or delegating or dropping an unwanted task, or deciding to make everything sacred, even sweeping the floor. Whatever you choose, choose to bring more joy and soul-nourishment into your life.

Use this space to journal about your experience with this Action Step:

"Know your own worth."

Journal Prompt: What I appreciate about myself is…

Merriam-Webster defines 'appreciate' as:

1. A) to grasp the nature, worth, quality, or significance of; B) to value or admire highly; C) to judge with heightened perception or understanding; to be fully aware of; D) to recognize with gratitude; and

2. to increase the value of…

Admittedly, the journal prompts in this section can seem almost interchangeable: I deserve, I love, I value, I appreciate, etc., and it is to be expected that your responses may be similar from exercise to exercise. Nonetheless, the different words carry slightly different meanings, and may spark different insights and touch different emotions. Savor the words, and see what each one brings up for you.

What I appreciate about myself is _____

I am so appreciative for my _____

What I appreciate about me is _____

Use this space to keep writing (use additional pages as needed):

Action Step:

Sing Praise!

Today the 'action' is our speech: I challenge you to say nice things about yourself! No agreement is needed from anyone else – simply state your truth, silently or out loud, if you dare! Some examples:

- ❖ I did a really good job with [fill in the blank].
- ❖ I have such a gift for [fill in the blank].
- ❖ Thank goodness I have the skill to [make this happen].
- ❖ Dang! I'm good!
- ❖ I declare myself Queen/Princess/President/CEO of [whatever I am doing].

Be extra supportive of yourself as you experiment with new ways of interacting with yourself and with the world. Remember, your effort is your success. And – just like playing the piano – everything gets easier with time and practice.

How did it feel? Note your responses.

Use this space to journal about your experience with this Action Step:

"No title can possibly confer any greater authority than that which you grant yourself."

Journal Prompt: What I like about myself is…

Include it all: I like my feet, I like my lips, I like the way I speak, my sense of humor, my strength, my caring, my kindness, my smile, my perseverance, my intelligence, etc.

It can feel almost shocking, can't it? We've gotten so used to viewing ourselves critically that it has become seemingly 'normal' to say the meanest things about ourselves, and seemingly 'abnormal' to like who we are. Let's turn this on its head – I mean right side up, where it belongs – and give ourselves the approval we deserve.

Special message for parents, teachers, relatives: do this for yourselves and for the children and teens in your life. They are so beautiful, and yet one of the most common phrases out of their mouths is "I hate my [fill in the blank]!" Help them by modeling self-love. They are worth it, and so are you!

What I like about myself is _____

What I like about me is _____

I like my _____

Use this space to keep writing (use additional pages as needed):

ACTION STEP:

A BIG PROMOTION!

I am pleased to inform you that you have been promoted to be the Boss of You! Congratulations! And – here's the thing – your only job, as Boss, is to encourage, support and approve of your every effort.

Have fun with it. If you make scrambled eggs, then pat yourself on the back for doing a good job; if the eggs drop on the floor, praise yourself for the effort.

Even if you can't stop worrying, well, just praise yourself for worrying. Your only job, as boss, is to praise and encourage the sole employee under your jurisdiction: you! Do everything that you imagine a good and encouraging boss would do to keep his or her prized employee happy.

This exercise may be just what we need to lighten up, have some fun, and love ourselves more. Notice how your new status as a super-fabulous, terrifically generous 'boss of you' affects you, and also influences those around you.

Use this space to journal about your experience with this Action Step:

"The work of our hands is a legacy to be cherished."

Journal Prompt: What I value about myself is…

This exercise is not limited to the work of your hands. This should take pages and pages – yes, you are that good!

In this, and in every exercise, allow the rhythm of your responses to flow: you might write in a rush, then slow down, then find a second, third and fourth wind. Give it a chance. Keep writing as long as there might be some 'juice' left – sometimes we have to dig a little for the pay dirt.

Any emotion that comes up is good. Tears and laughter wash away sadness, and clear space for new experiences to come.

What I value about myself is _____

What I value about myself is _____

What I value about myself is _____

Use this space to keep writing (use additional pages as needed):

ACTION STEP:

FIND AN OBJECT

Choose a small object to represent one quality that you value about yourself. The object can be something you find around your home, or in nature, or in a shop. It can be a mug, a stone, a note, a poem, a piece of jewelry, an article of clothing, or anything else you choose.

Hold that object and say: "I am so precious."

Keep the object near you or on your person all day. Look at it, touch it throughout the day to remind you of how valuable and precious you are.

Use this space to journal about your experience with this Action Step:

"Never allow any aspect of a project to betray your hard work or intentions."

Journal Prompt: The way I support my efforts is…

Our efforts deserve our full talent and support. Our 'efforts' can mean anything important to us, from getting to the White House, to just getting through the day.

One of my favorite stories is that of Queen Esther, who had to approach the king to make a request – something that was punishable by death if the king did not accept her approach. She fasted and prayed for three days before approaching the king, and asked all her handmaidens and all her people to fast and pray with her – only then did she approach the king. (Spoiler alert – it worked!) This exemplifies the idea of supporting our efforts. She did everything in her power, and then some, in order to lay the groundwork for the success of her mission.

Write all the ways you support your goals and dreams.

The way I support my efforts is _____

I support my efforts by _____

I support my efforts when _____

Use this space to keep writing (use additional pages as needed):

ACTION STEP:

COMPLETION

Ann always said: "complete your work with finesse." She didn't want us go to the trouble of knitting a sweater, only to sew on the buttons carelessly, or wash it incorrectly.

Today, complete one thing. Wrap up a bit of unfinished business.

It can be small or large. It can be writing a check, mailing a letter, making a phone call, sewing a button, or cleaning a sock drawer. If you don't have time to clean a whole drawer, then just fold one item and put it away nicely. The point is to complete a task.

When you are done, give yourself a pat yourself on the back and a hearty "well done!" Success builds on success. Completing one thing with joy and satisfaction will lead to many more accomplishments.

Use this space to journal about your experience with this Action Step:

"Do it right and wear it with pride."

Journal Prompt: I feel proud of me when…

"Do it right and wear it with pride" was Ann's motto. She took the time to think through what she thought was the best way to approach a thing, and, after that, she felt supremely confident in her choices.

It is said that 'pride goes before a fall' (*Proverbs 16:18*), yet many of us suffer from the opposite problem, that of *not* taking pride in ourselves. When a child takes pride in a new accomplishment, it encourages growth. Ann's pride, too, was all to the good, for it gave her the confidence that she had something valuable to share with others.

What makes YOU feel proud? Go ahead, be proud of you!

I feel proud of me when _____

I feel proud of the way I _____

I am proud that _____

Use this space to keep writing (use additional pages as needed):

ACTION STEP:

DECLARE VICTORY AND MOVE ON

We face big and small decisions all day. Do you allow other people to sway you to abandon your original desire? Do you second guess yourself? Do you get 'buyer's remorse'?

Today, dial down on the self-questioning, and dial up on feeling good. Decide about issues as they come up (even if you decide to postpone making a decision!), declare victory, and move on. To the best of your ability, don't dwell on your decisions, and practice feeling confident about your choices.

Here are some additional ways to flex your decision-making muscle:

❖ Wear an article of clothing you haven't had the courage to wear yet.

❖ Style something with new flair: wear a scarf around your waist instead of your neck; use a sweater as a scarf; pile on six necklaces, three watches and ten bracelets; etc. Decide not to care about what other people think about it. As my spiritual teacher, Shanta, used to say: "Your opinion of me is none of my business!"

❖ Change your environment: choose a new paint color, rearrange the furniture, etc.

❖ Change the order in which you habitually do things, or do something out of the ordinary: treat yourself to something posh, or begin a meal with dessert – break the mold.

Use this space to journal about your experience with this Action Step.

"Your voice is needed."

Journal Prompt: What I like about my story is…

Using your life as your 'material,' what kind of a story would your life tell?

For example, without any self-consciousness or self-censorship, imagine: if you were a hero, and your journey was a 'hero's tale,' what would it look like? Or, do you see yourself as a warrior? If so, describe your mission. Or, a princess? A queen? A shaman? A wise woman? A tigress? An innocent child? An adventurer?

What kind of story would your life be?

What I like about my story is _____

My life is a story of _____

My story is like _____

Use this space to keep writing (use additional pages as needed):

ACTION STEP:

LOVE YOUR EXPRESSION

Self-consciousness can infiltrate our most private moments, even when writing in a journal ("Am I allowed to feel what I am feeling, think what I am thinking, or say what I want to say?") or standing in front of a blank canvas ("Can I really paint what I want?).

Today, take a blank piece of paper, some pens, pencils, markers or paint, and... do something! Anything! Let it out. Paint or sketch or write – just put your mark to paper: dots, scribbles, lines, words, sketches – it's all good.

Whatever you do, mess or masterpiece (do not judge which it is!), look at your paper and speak these three phrases:

❖ I see you just the way you are.

❖ I accept you just the way you are.

❖ I am proud of you just the way you are.

How does it feel? Can you imagine ways to apply this to your day-to-day life?

Use this space to journal about your experience with this Action Step:

"There are things that want to be said."

Journal Prompt: My message is…

What is the message that defines you? What, in your heart of hearts, is the message you would like to put out into the world? What is the message you need to hear?

My message is _____

What I want to say is _____

The message my heart wants to say is _____

Use this space to keep writing (use additional pages as needed):

ACTION STEP:

YOUR MESSAGE X 2

Make double sure that your message comes across. Deliver your message once, and then deliver it again.

We tend to assume that our message is understood. We think, "I cook for my family, therefore they must understand that I do this as an expression of love." However, that may not be true. Once, a mother saw her little boy about to be run over by a car. With a heroic leap, she tackled him to the ground and saved his life. However, he did not see the oncoming car; he only felt his mother roughly knock him to the ground. This misperception planted seeds of mistrust that stayed with him the rest of his life.

Make sure YOUR message is clear. Do the action *and* speak your truth: "I do this because I care for my family." "I did this deal for the betterment of the company." "I painted this to inspire hope."

Though this might feel awkward at first, just do your best – the payoff is huge. When you recognize your own best efforts, then others, too, will give your efforts the recognition they deserve.

Use this space to journal about your experience with this Action Step:

"Your truth, too, has a voice, a strand in the fabric."

Journal Prompt: From my heart, I want to say…

What is in your heart? What wants to be said? It helps to place a hand over your heart as you write.

From my heart, I want to say _____

From my heart, it is important for me to say _____

From my heart, I say _____

Use this space to keep writing (use additional pages as needed):

ACTION STEP:

DANCE YOUR TRUTH

Sometimes we speak with our words. Sometimes we express ourselves through color and design, a creative project, or a delicious meal. And sometimes we speak with our bodies, so…

Let's give ourselves that gift. Put on some music, and dance!

Dance your truth. Dance gentle, dance hard, dance sexy, sassy, slow or fast, or just wave your arms in the air. Let your spirit move you. Express yourself. Celebrate yourself.

We are each so very beautiful. *You* are so very beautiful. Let go, and dance!

Use this space to journal about your experience with this Action Step:

*"Unwind the myths, unravel the illusions,
and arrive at a core of truth."*

Journal Prompt: My life is asking me to notice…

Look back over the past week as if watching a movie. Are there things that stand out for you as an annoyance, a challenge, or a delight? What are the themes that are presenting themselves in your current experience?

My life is asking me to notice _____

I see a pattern of _____

My life is asking me to notice _____

Use this space to keep writing (use additional pages as needed):

ACTION STEP:

TAKE A MINI-VACATION

Today, reconnect with happiness, joy, ease, pleasure, relaxation, and all those delicious holiday feelings, even in the midst of your busy life.

❖ If you have time, go somewhere – forest, beach, or town. Carry as little as possible. Have no agenda, simply follow the flow. Allow your desires to lead you.

❖ Or, enjoy a 'staycation' – take a relaxing bath, or a walk, or do nothing at all. Just remind yourself that you are officially 'on vacation' for a period of time and see what happens.

❖ If you have no time to take a private moment, then create a vacation mindset in the midst of whatever you are doing. For caregivers, this might mean walking behind a baby carriage or a wheelchair, or perhaps inviting your kids to play along with your 'fantasy vacation' game.

For five minutes or five hours, be happy. Allow yourself a worry-free period; enter an anger-free zone. Drop the cares, and relax. Let go the need to do, or accomplish anything, and give yourself permission to just be.

Notice how it feels. And notice how your mini-vacation influenced the rest of your day.

Use this space to journal about your experience with this Action Step:

"What is my story?"

Journal Prompt: This year, my life is asking me to notice…

Look back over the past year as if you are watching a movie. Are there things that stand out for you as an annoyance, a challenge, growth, or delight? What are the themes that presented themselves to you the past year?

This year, my life is asking me to notice _____

This year, the theme of my life is _____

My life is asking me to notice _____

Use this space to keep writing (use additional pages as needed):

ACTION STEP:

A CHANGE IN PERSPECTIVE

Life can be seen as a spiral. Each time we travel the spiral, our experiences feel familiar, yet, in truth, we are on a higher level than the previous time around.

For example, a woman with multiple divorces may have a first divorce that included alimony, property and custody battles; a second divorce with property conflicts, but no alimony or custody battles; and a third divorce that is amicable. Far from being 'stuck in a rut,' the woman is mastering one of life's experiences. Each time she passes through a divorce there is less struggle, until she has mastered the essential aspects of the experience.

This perspective gives us the opportunity to see the good in our challenging experiences. Consider viewing the challenges in your life (and we all have them), through this lens. Note your progress; praise yourself for learning; applaud your growth. Remember that you are mastering life's lessons.

Learning isn't always pretty; every Olympic skater has had their share of falls. Recognize that – far from being in a rut - you are on a path of mastery. Well done, you!

Use this space to journal about your experience with this Action Step:

> *"We matter to each other in ways*
> *we may never fully understand."*

Journal Prompt: I matter when I...

Write *all* the ways you contribute to life and to those around you. Do not hold back!

Go to town on this one: list everything you do, from the smile you share, to organizing an event (big or small), to calling a friend in need, to kissing a skinned knee – everything! You are so awesome!

I matter when I _____

I make a difference when I _____

I contribute when I _____

Use this space to keep writing (use additional pages as needed):

ACTION STEP:

ALLOW YOUR VALUE TO STAND

Do your words negate your value? "Oh, anyone could have done that!" "It's no big deal." "I just did a little." "If I didn't do it, someone else would have done it." "I should have done more." "I could have done better."

What matters is not that someone else could have done what you did, or that you weren't the best, or that it wasn't well received, or that it was a small thing, or that it was incomplete. All that matters is that YOU DID IT … THAT IS WHAT MATTERS!

Allow your value to stand. No excuses, no apologies, no minimizing.

This is HUGE. It could be a life-changer.

Tip: the habit of negative self-talk can be so ingrained that it might be fun to set up a reward system to help implement a new self-loving habit: every time you refrain from saying something negative about yourself, put a quarter or a dollar in a jar, to spend as you wish. Enjoy your accomplishment, and enjoy your rewards!

Use this space to journal about your experience with this Action Step:

"Ann saw the good in others."

Journal Prompt: I see the good in me…

A friend recently told me about an experiment: An artist sat facing away from a participant and had the participant describe himself. Based on the person's verbal description, the artist painted the participant's portrait. Next, a different participant described the first participant, and the artist painted the first participant's portrait again, this time based on the other person's description of him. He did this many times, and then exhibited the pairs of paintings side by side.

The result? The portraits based on the self-descriptions highlighted 'flaws,' whereas the portraits based on the other person's description highlighted the person's best qualities.

Seek out your good qualities. Stop focusing on the 'flaws,' and see the good in you.

I see the good in me _____

I see the good in me when _____

What is so good about me is _____

Use this space to keep writing (use additional pages as needed):

ACTION STEP:

DECLARE IT GOOD

In the beginning…it was good.

There was no talk of "It's not done yet," or "Come back when it's finished," or "Wait until tomorrow, then it'll be good." At every stage of creation, it was 'good.'

Whatever you do today – be it funky or fabulous – approve of your work.

In the previous Action Step, you allowed your contributions to stand, with no excuses, and no apologies. Today, take it a step further by positively supporting your value. Declare your actions "good." Be pleased with your effort. At every stage of creation – be it unfinished, imperfect, or whatever – say: "I did this, and it is good."

It takes courage and persistence to change a habit. Kudos and blue ribbons to you for taking these powerful steps in self-love.

Keep that reward jar open! This time, reward yourself every time you make a positive comment about yourself. In fact, double your reward for this huge step forward in positive self-talk.

Use this space to journal about your experience with this Action Step:

"A hallmark of a generous teacher
is the ability to step into a beginner's shoes."

Journal Exercise: My heart feels open when…

What softens your heart? When do you feel relaxed enough and safe enough to allow your heart to be open?

What does it mean to you to say that 'your heart is open'?

I feel compassion when _____

I heart opens when _____

When my heart is open I feel _____

Use this space to keep writing (use additional pages as needed):

ACTION STEP:

LET IT BE

Today's action step is non-action. Sometimes, we mistake compassion for jumping in and fixing someone else's problem, or apologizing for it, or compensating for it, or taking it on in some other way. Today we will compassionately allow the other person's issue to be his or her issue, not ours.

Truthfully, this is not non-action, rather, it is the subtle action of standing in our truth and allowing others to stand in their truth as well. It is not the indifference of "It's your problem," but the generosity of "I see what you are going through." Granting another person the space to be where he or she is may be the greatest gift we can offer.

Doing nothing can be challenging. To stand in the face of another's pain, anger or discomfort can feel intensely uncomfortable to the person witnessing it. Let it be. Let others be who they are – they will be, anyway! Let them have their experience – they have the tools to handle their challenges, if they want to. Let the act of witnessing be like a wave that washes over you, and know that calmer waters will follow any rough currents.

We stand to reclaim so much of our own vitality when we develop a clearer picture of what belongs to us, and what belongs to another. Today's mantra: "Let it be!"

Use this space to journal about your experience with this Action Step:

"Teaching creates a meeting ground, a bridge to others."

Journal Exercise: I open to others when…

Teaching means not just sharing information, but also sharing who we are. It is not *what* we do, but rather the *way* we do it, that transmits the real message we impart to others.

Whether we are in a kitchen, office, classroom, or any other setting, the essence of who we are can be an inspiration to others.

I open to others when _____

I feel my heart open to others when _____

I share who I am with others when _____

Use this space to keep writing (use additional pages as needed):

ACTION STEP:

TRUTH TELLING

The truth works. Today, when you are engaged in conversation, or you've been asked to do something, before responding, place your hand over your heart and say "The truth is…" and state your truth.

It is terrifically empowering to know that the stickiest situations can be resolved by stating the truth. Trust the truth.

Things we think would be 'too much' to say often turn out to be perfectly acceptable. If you don't want to do something, instead of spending time and energy dreaming up excuses and feeling uncomfortable, try: "The truth is, I don't want to."

Use this space to journal about your experience with this Action Step:

"Ann did not teach life lessons, per se,
her wisdom was all applied."

Journal Exercise: I want my actions to say...

What do you stand for? What is your message? What do you hope people understand from your actions?

Write to help clarify your vision and empower your intentions.

I want my actions to say _____

I want my actions to say _____

My actions say _____

Use this space to keep writing (use additional pages as needed):

ACTION STEP:

MANIFESTING OPPORTUNITY

On a piece of paper, write: "Today, I find the opportunity to…" [complete the sentence with what you wish to have the opportunity to do].

If you write your note at night, tuck it in a pajama pocket, or under your pillow or mattress, or keep it close by on your night table. The following day, carry the note all day (ladies – tucking the note in your bra is a great way to keep it close). When you have a private moment, take it out and reread it. If you write your note in the morning, simply carry it or wear it on your person that same day.

Note any interesting occurrences that happen for you throughout the day. Did being on the lookout for those opportunities make you more aware? How did it feel?

Use this space to journal about your experience with this Action Step:

"Ann's presence — that gift to us of her time and energy — was the subtext of every lesson."

Journal Exercise: I feel most present when...

Ann loved sharing her passion for knitting. She was a volunteer at the Y, where I met her, and even when she was a high school speech teacher, you can bet she taught all her students – male and female – to knit.

Sometimes we just have to create our own opportunities to do what we love. If we want to star in a movie, sometimes we just have to write, produce and star in our own movie! The first step, however, is to know what we love.

What do you love to do? What floats your boat? What makes you feel most alive? What gives your life meaning? When do you feel most present?

I feel most present when _____

I feel most fully alive when _____

The thing I love to do most is _____

Use this space to keep writing (use additional pages as needed):

ACTION STEP:

CULTIVATING JOY

Doing more of what you love is a simple path to more joy.

A journey of a thousand miles starts with a single step. Take a step closer to what you love.

For example, if being around animals makes you happy, then explore ways to bring more of that into your life: volunteer at an animal shelter, zoo, or other animal-related facility, train for a career working with animals, etc.

Similarly, if you feel happiest involved in the creative arts, then join an art class or club, volunteer to help paint scenery for your local high school theater productions, or just start painting or doodling with magic markers.

Make a phone call, do research online, or visit a location. Start small or go big, your choice, as long as you take a step toward what you love.

Use this space to journal about your experience with this Action Step:

"Do not keep your gifts to yourself.
The right people will be there to receive your message."

Journal Exercise: What I value most about my contribution is…

Each of our contributions is uniquely valuable, because we each filter our expression through the prism of our personalities and experience, and there are those that need to hear our message in just the way we express it.

Some people 'speak' music, art, dance, or writing, or a combination of several forms of expression. Perhaps your gift is baking, sewing, or matchmaking. What do you 'speak'?

What are your gifts? What is your expression?

I value that I offer the gift of _____

*I value my gifts most when I*_____

My most valuable gifts are _____

Use this space to keep writing (use additional pages as needed):

ACTION STEP:

TURNING STRAW INTO GOLD

Today we will perform a magical alchemical experiment in transmuting straw into gold. I know! I know! I promised there'd be no mystical hocus pocus! Nonetheless, we've been together long enough to do a little experiment, right?

The key to today's experiment is the notion that everything has two sides. We shall see the positive side of something we usually accept as a 'negative.' For example, instead of accepting a label of 'pushover,' I will call it kindness and gentleness; if I am known for my temper, I will value it as passion and strength; if I am 'pushy,' I will re-define it as committed and caring.

When I value my gifts, I can exercise them appropriately. For instance, if I value my passion, then I am more likely to take a stand for what I care about – and I no longer need to wait for it to build into an explosion. Respecting myself as determined, rather than pushy, moves interactions to an entirely new level: "I feel strongly about this because I care about you" is a far cry from "My way or the highway!" When I value my gentleness, I am better able to bestow it when and where I choose, rather than regret it as a 'weakness.'

You really are golden, you are just brushing off the straw and allowing the gold to shine forth. It is not really so mysterious, but it is quite magical.

Use this space to journal about your experience with this Action Step:

"In life, as in knitting, do not leave loose ends."

Journal Exercise: If I tied up some loose ends I would...

Take a loving look around: is your mind full of unfinished business, or your home full of unfinished projects?

Are there some that you can let go?

Are there some you could wrap up?

What would happen if you tied up some of the loose ends? What work do you wish to focus on? What would happen if there were fewer projects on your "To do" list?

How does this exercise feel? Take a deep breath, relax, and allow answers and images to come to you.

If I tied up some loose ends I would _____

If I let go a project I would feel _____

When I think about my unfinished projects I feel _____

Use this space to keep writing (use additional pages as needed):

ACTION STEP:

DE-CLUTTERING THE MIND

Is your life 'telling you something?' Take a moment, and listen.

For example, on the day I wrote this, I closed my eyes and looked at what life was sending me. I saw myself as so busy, with so many projects to complete, and so much to take care of. I felt a little like the White Rabbit in *Alice in Wonderland*: "I'm late, I'm late, for a very important date!"

Instead of allowing this nervous energy to buzz like an annoying gnat in the back of my mind, I took a deep breath, and took a good look at it. Here's how the process went:

I ask myself, can I redefine it? ("Thank heavens I have so many meaningful projects and relationships; this is the life I have chosen and I gratefully accept all that comes with it.") Or do I need to take action? ("I need to find a way to simplify my life so that I can spend more time doing the things that are most meaningful to me.") Is there a gift in what I see as a stress? ("These projects allow me to practice faith in the face of so many unknowns.")

Just like clutter clearing a home, instead of using mental energy to *ignore* the pile of clothes in the corner, take a moment to focus on the pile, shake out each item, and decide whether to love it and put it back in the closet, or let it go, and put it in a bag and out the door.

As you think about what your life is 'telling' you, see which ideas boost your energy. Feel what approach helps you more joyfully handle what life is presenting you.

Use this space to journal about your experience with this Action Step:

"I am part of a chain of skill that has been handed down for generations."

Journal Exercise: I am so grateful for…

What is your inheritance? What are your gifts? What are you grateful for?

Look not just to your family ancestors, but to all the people and experiences that have guided and enriched your life. Look around you, and look within you. From the basics of food and shelter, to the deepest life lessons, it is good to acknowledge what has been given.

I am grateful for _____

I give thanks for _____

I am full of gratitude for _____

Use this space to keep writing (use additional pages as needed):

ACTION STEP:

YES, THANK YOU

All the kind words in the world are meaningless unless we believe them. All the most wonderful gifts are as dust unless we accept them.

No one can give you anything unless you first allow yourself to receive it.

Open your heart to the gifts that are there in such abundance for you. Say "yes, thank you," to all the goodness and kindness coming your way.

Most importantly, say yes to yourself. Open your heart and allow the goodness in.

How much can you say yes to today?

Yes. Yes. Yes, thank you!

Use this space to journal about your experience with this Action Step:

"You can't pick the flowers without taking the walk."

Journal Exercise: I wish I were brave enough to...

If you were unafraid, what would you do?

I wish I were brave enough to _____

If I were unafraid, I would _____

When I am unafraid, I feel _____

Use this space to keep writing (use additional pages as needed):

ACTION STEP:

COURAGE!

Today, do one brave thing. For one person, it may take courage to walk into a restaurant or cinema alone, for another it may take courage to call someone and invite them along; what might be easy for one person could be a brave act for someone else. Wherever we start from, when we stretch our limits, we strengthen our capability. Bit by bit, we can do great things.

Part Two of this exercise is to reward yourself for your act of courage. This can be as simple as self-acknowledgement, or it can be a physical reward, like having a dessert, or a massage, or whatever treat makes you feel totally pampered and rewarded.

For some of us, the self-approval might be the part of the exercise that takes the most courage. Do you dare to think you are terrific? Are you brave enough to give yourself unqualified approval?

If it felt a little uncomfortable, it's OK to acknowledge that, as long as you also find the positive things to praise as well. Courage, self-care, growth, daring, self-approval, honesty and self-acceptance are all part of your experience today.

Use this space to journal about your experience with this Action Step:

"Learn together and learn from one another."

Journal Exercise: I Share With Others...

My knitting teacher, Ann, had a gift to cut through the walls that separate us. She touched people in a deeply personal way: she stood up for her car service driver in court, she guided her local yarn store manager through his family's adoption process, she helped a student get settled in a new neighborhood, she cured someone else of a lisp where no other therapist had been able to help (she was by profession a H.S. speech teacher), and she entrusted me with her story, which was the catalyst for my journey of self-love.

The way Ann touched people's lives had nothing to do with college degrees or being in a 'power position to effect change.' *Being alive* was Ann's 'power position,' and *life* is where she found the people who needed her particular gifts.

We bring so much to each other when we open up to one another. What areas of your life or interests might you like to share with others? What would you enjoy sharing?

I would like to share _____

My dream of community is _____

I wish to work with others to _____

Use this space to keep writing (use additional pages as needed):

ACTION STEP:

OPENING TO OTHERS

Share generously of yourself today. This may be in the context of something you always do, or it can be something out of the ordinary. For example, if you always meet a friend for coffee, then make it special; really be present and share the time and the experience to the fullest. Or, you can initiate a new project entirely.

Whatever it is, you do not have to complete it, or do it perfectly, you just have to do something. Simply initiate the process.

The intention of this exercise is not to 'force' any generosity that you do not feel. Rather, the idea is that sharing who you are is a gift to YOU. It is *for you*, not the other person (it is that, too, but that is secondary). There is something wonderful about allowing ourselves to be who we are, and allowing our gifts to shine.

What will you share of yourself today? What is one thing you can do to move yourself toward sharing your gifts with others?

Use this space to journal about your experience with this Action Step:

"The gifts can only be released by doing the task."

Journal Exercise: The gift I would most like is…

What would make your life 'perfect'? What is your definition of your best life?

What does your best life look like?

The gift I would most like is _____

What I wish for most in my life is _____

The gift I'd most like to receive is _____

Use this space to keep writing (use additional pages as needed):

ACTION STEP:

ACCEPTING A STARRING ROLE

Imagine that you are the star of your own movie. Though it sounds frightfully ego-centric, just for a moment, imagine that everything in your life is there for the sole purpose of advancing your story. Imagine that the annoying boss or pesky neighbor or troubled teen in your life is actually an angel in disguise, specifically here for the purpose of offering you new challenges and bringing you the teachings you need.

Far from encouraging raving egomaniacs, I think this exercise helps build joy, love and compassion. For, if that troubled teen or pesky neighbor in my life is really is an angel in disguise, I would turn to him or her with different eyes. I would see through their surface annoyances and bless their presence in my life as a part of the whole beautiful creation that is my life, there to be part of my 'movie' and facilitate my growth. This attitude can help us grow in love and compassion, for others and for ourselves, every day.

What does each situation in your life offer you? Pick one situation that perhaps troubles you, and, as an exercise, regard the players in this situation as angels. What gifts are these angels bringing you? What action would these angels most like to see you take?

Use this space to journal about your experience with this Action Step:

"The doing and the daring are the magic keys
to unlocking the treasure chest."

Journal Exercise: My big dream is...

Let your imagination run wild. What would you be doing right now if this was your 'dream life'? Write down your biggest, most ambitious dreams.

Give yourself permission to be completely uninhibited as you write your dreams, whether or not they are 'realistic.'

My greatest dream would be _____

My big dream is _____

My fantasy dream is _____

Use this space to keep writing (use additional pages as needed):

ACTION STEP:

LOVE YOUR NOW

Loving your NOW is the key to creating a happy life.

I used to teach dance in a large studio in NYC. Over time, I became dissatisfied with some things about the job, and that began to affect my mood and my attitude. I hate to admit it, but I felt quite the victim. When I became aware of what was happening, I changed gears. Instead of focusing on the negative, I focused on what I loved about the job, and it turned out there was a lot to love. I felt privileged to work in a field I adored, with fun co-workers, surrounded by music and dance, swimming in a sea of creativity. Wow! What a switch. I was suddenly in love with the place.

The funny thing is, I was just as suddenly out of there. Within a year I started my own dance studio; energetically, it felt as though one scene simply melted away and another rose up in its place. When I was unhappy, I felt 'trapped'; my new attitude opened the door for me to move on to the next experience.

If there is a situation in your life that you're not completely happy with, for this exercise, ignore the bits you aren't so thrilled with, and focus on what you appreciate or love about it. Put blinders on and only see the positive.

Success builds on success. Love your NOW; it is the key to your future!

Use this space to journal about your experience with this Action Step:

"Learning to follow the yarn is the biggest gift of all."

Journal Exercise: I trust…

The universe is looking out for us, providing us with whatever we need, guiding us with the utmost kindness. Even our challenges are there for us: they are forces for good, guiding us, protecting us and helping us along the way.

This attitude may seem foreign at first; nonetheless, it becomes stronger as we welcome a sense of 'spirit' into our lives. As we become more aware of the loving forces in our lives, our burdens are lightened. We are no longer going it alone.

I trust that _____

I feel trust that _____

*I feel trusting when*_____

Use this space to keep writing (use additional pages as needed):

ACTION STEP:

BEING SUPPORTED

Take a moment to notice yourself sitting in your chair. Feel your chair supporting you, holding you, cradling you. Allow your body to rest and be held by the chair.

As you walk around your house, feel the support of the ground beneath you. Feel your feet on the earth (even if you are in a high-rise many floors above the ground).

Turn on the tap, see how the water flows for you. Have a drink, and notice how the cup holds the liquid for you.

As you breath in and out, observe that the air is there for you, and notice the wondrous working of all the systems of your body, taking in air, circulating the oxygen, supplying you with energy and vitality, supporting your life.

Take a walk, even just around your block. As you walk, step by step, feel your connection to the ground beneath your feet. It is holding you up, supporting you with every step you take. How does it feel?

Use this space to journal about your experience with this Action Step:

"Enjoy the journey."

Journal Exercise: I applaud myself when...

It is time to stop looking towards the pot of gold at the end of the rainbow and start enjoying our romp on this multi-colored arc of road called LIFE, i.e., it is time to stop thinking so much about the destination, and focus more on the journey. Let's celebrate our efforts, rather than our accomplishments. In other words, our effort IS our accomplishment.

Instead of waiting for the 'big days,' such as graduations, weddings, promotions, etc., celebrate the little things. Success builds on success, and happiness builds on happiness. See the worthiness of everything you do. You do so much, so beautifully, so generously, and so caringly. Do not wait for a 'big day.' Today is the day to notice and applaud you.

I applaud myself today for _____

I celebrate this about myself _____

I celebrate my efforts today _____

Use this space to keep writing (use additional pages as needed):

ACTION STEP:

SELF-ADORNMENT

Be the Queen of Sheba. Put on something that makes you feel special and wonderful. You are so beautiful!

Don't save your 'special things' for 'special days.' You decide which days are 'special.' Declare today a celebration of YOU!

I cordially invite you to step over to your closet, your dresser, or your jewelry box, and adorn yourself. Take it up a notch (or two or three). Enjoy the beauty of YOU.

Use this space to journal about your experience with this Action Step:

"Yarn speaks volumes, even when whispering a lullaby."

Journal Exercise: I have quiet faith that...

There is great strength in gentleness. Sometimes we get so swept up in the excitement of volume, speed, and flash, that we can lose sight of the quiet glow of contentment, love, peace and faith.

Quiet faith in who we are and where we are going will carry us very, very far.

I have quiet faith that _____

I have faith that _____

I know that _____

Use this space to keep writing (use additional pages as needed):

ACTION STEP:

MY CUP RUNNETH OVER

In your kitchen sink, place a large platter. On top of that, place a dinner plate. On top of that, a lunch plate, and on top of that, a saucer. Next, place a soup bowl, and, finally, on top of that, a cup.

Next, take a pitcher of water, and begin pouring *only* into the cup. Notice how as the cup overflows, it spills over into the bowl, and from there it cascades into the saucer, and from there to the lunch plate, etc.

You are the cup. If you start by pouring water into the platter, it will never reach the cup. Yet when you fill the cup, your cup will run over, and bring goodness to all the people in your life, overflowing from you to your family, to your friends, to your community, to your city, to your state, to your country, to the whole world.

Fill your cup!

I encourage you to get up and actually do this one. You may eventually forget these words, but you will never forget seeing with your own eyes how the water that is poured into your own cup overflows and fills everything around it.

Use this space to journal about your experience with this Action Step:

"Seek out the positive in every situation."

Journal Exercise: I deserve…

We return to the first exercise.

We seek out the positive in every situation, and, most importantly, we seek out the positive in ourselves. This is self-love: to see ourselves with the eyes of kindness, caring, compassion, generosity, and understanding. It is the beginning of healing, and of happiness.

You are good, you are fine, you are deserving. You are the most important person in your life. What you choose for yourself is what matters. What do you claim for yourself?

I deserve _____

I believe I deserve _____

I claim that I deserve _____

Use this space to keep writing (use additional pages as needed):

ACTION STEP:

A VALENTINE

Write yourself a love letter. Get a piece of paper, and write yourself the most loving, encouraging, kind and understanding message you possibly can write. Sing your praise, applaud your efforts. Write all the words your heart needs to hear.

Sign the letter, put it in an envelope, seal it, and tuck it in a safe place.

Use this space to journal about your experience with this Action Step:

"May you be fortunate to find a teacher
who makes your heart sing."

Journal Exercise: I would like to bring into my life...

To me, my teachers are my riches. They have lifted me up, and I am so grateful.

What are *your* riches? What abundance do you wish for?

You deserve the best! What do you wish to bring into your life? For the exercise, let go any 'practical' objections or considerations (money, time, etc.) and just write.

I would like to bring into my life _____

I deserve to have in my life _____

I would like to explore _____

Use this space to keep writing (use additional pages as needed):

ACTION STEP:

RECEIVING

Open the letter you wrote to yourself yesterday. Enjoy this gift of love from yourself.

It is wonderful to know that you are loved, embraced, and cherished by the most important person in your life - YOU!

You are beautiful, amazing, unique, powerful and wondrous.

You are loved, embraced, and cherished.

You have done so much to strengthen your happiness habits, and you are on the way to greater self-love. As you allow more self-love, you are allowing ALL the love in your life to flow.

Keep your letter as a reminder of how dear you are. Re-read it often. Give yourself the gift of repeating this exercise whenever you need a reminder of how wonderful, beautiful, and cherished you are.

Remember, remember, remember, always, that you are loved.

Use this space to journal about your experience with this Action Step:

BOOKS BY REBA LINKER

Amazon Kindle #1 Bestseller - **Follow the Yarn: The Knitting Wit & Wisdom of Ann Sokolowski**

"The author shares the gift of her heart, wide open. Instruction, inspiration and love — all in one delightful package." — Marcy Nelson-Garrison, The PINK Paradigm

"This is a how-to-knit book, yes, but more importantly a story of healing and inspiring wisdom." — Marilyn Graman, Lifeworks

"Reba's clear, luminous style smoothly combines Ann Sokolowski's encyclopedic knowledge of knitting with lively, humorous anecdotes. *Follow the Yarn* is a fitting tribute to a master teacher and a one-of kind-woman." — Gail Straub, Empowerment Institute

The Little Book of Manifesting Big!

Unleash the power of your own mind to create all that you desire! *The Little Book of Manifesting Big!* brings clarity, humor, and beauty to the topic of manifesting your best life.

"*The Little Book of Manifesting Big* takes on a huge topic and makes it simple, manageable, and doable. In it, Reba Linker shows how we truly do create our own reality!" — Jodi Chapman, SoulSpeak.com

… so clear, so simple, so readable, so encouraging…and it makes it all so easy! Thank you!" — Karen Packwood, The Truth Whisperer

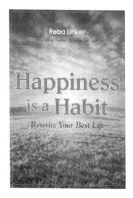

Happiness is a Habit: Rewrite Your Best Life

Happiness is a Habit takes an in-depth look at how to create your best and happiest life. It weaves a rich tapestry of stories, spiritual wisdom, personal anecdotes, and practical exercises.

Happiness is a Habit is due out in summer 2015 as an e-book and in print.

Visit **www.RebaLinker.com/books/** to learn more.

A NOTE FROM THE AUTHOR

I am honored to be part of your path to greater self-love. I wish you happiness and success. It is a journey, not a destination, and you are very much on your way!

Let's travel further together; I am a teacher, a guide, and a coach, and I am ready to lead you to a more fulfilled life. Group coaching and courses are a great way to share our laughter and tears, our challenges and victories. I am also available for private coaching. Find out more about working with me at http://rebalinker.com/transformational-coaching/

Imagine Self-Love is available on Amazon Kindle. If you enjoyed *Imagine Self-Love*, I would be grateful if you would leave a review at Amazon.com.

I would love to know which quotes and exercises worked best for you. Your input will help improve the journal for future participants. You can contact me directly at Reba@RebaLinker.com or on Facebook at 'Reba Linker, Author/Coach.'

To learn more about private coaching, courses, and books, and to sign up and become part of the *Walks with Spirit* community, please visit http://www.RebaLinker.com.

Blessings, *Reba*

Made in the USA
San Bernardino, CA
30 June 2015